BIRTH OF A
SUPERHERO

MICHELLE NOLD

BALBOA.
PRESS

A DIVISION OF HAY HOUSE

Balboa Press books may be ordered through booksellers or by contacting:

Balboa Press
A Division of Hay House
1663 Liberty Drive
Bloomington, IN 47403
www.balboapress.com
1 (877) 407-4847

Because of the dynamic nature of the Internet, any web addresses or links contained in this book may have changed since publication and may no longer be valid. The views expressed in this work are solely those of the author and do not necessarily reflect the views of the publisher, and the publisher hereby disclaims any responsibility for them.

The author of this book does not dispense medical advice or prescribe the use of any technique as a form of treatment for physical, emotional, or medical problems without the advice of a physician, either directly or indirectly. The intent of the author is only to offer information of a general nature to help you in your quest for emotional and spiritual well-being. In the event you use any of the information in this book for yourself, which is your constitutional right, the author and the publisher assume no responsibility for your actions.

Any people depicted in stock imagery provided by Thinkstock are models, and such images are being used for illustrative purposes only. Certain stock imagery © Thinkstock.

Print information available on the last page.

ISBN: 978-1-5043-6955-8 (sc)
ISBN: 978-1-5043-6956-5 (e)

Library of Congress Control Number: 2016918658

Balboa Press rev. date: 11/04/2016

Oh what a tangled web we weave

When first we practice to deceive

—Sir Walter Scott

ACKNOWLEDGEMENTS

This book is dedicated to my husband, Rick, who was instrumental in making me into the woman I am today.
Special Acknowledgements
To my dear friends, Genie, Sue, and Joe Dee, whose constant support and encouragement fueled my desire to pursue a career as a public speaker.

Special Thanks

To Karen Smith's talented guidance, without which this book would not have been possible.

It is with profound gratitude and respect that I thank you all.

TABLE OF CONTENTS

PREFACE

Deception comes in many forms, but not all deception is born out of malice. In my life it came in the form of seemingly harmless tales told to me when I was young and impressionable. In my later years, deception reared its seductive head each time I tried to fulfill a goal or satisfy a personal ambition. I became a story teller. I told myself stories like "It isn't meant to be". I bought into the philosophy of "You can't do that" until I hit an emotional rock bottom and had an epiphany. Now I tell myself a different story. Charles R. Swindoll said that, "Life is 10% what happens to you and 90% how you react to it." I chose not to react but to design.

Within the pages of this book you will discover what I learned in this moment of my epiphany. We are all designers. We have a power unlike anything else in the world. "Beneath the rule of men entirely great, the pen is mightier than the sword" was written by Edward Bulwer Lytton, English novelist, poet, playwright and politician in his play Cardinal Richelieu in 1839.

My life has taught me that I have the power to craft my life how I want, to fulfill my hopes and dreams once I realized the key.

INTRODUCTION

This once vast orb so warm and soft; now narrows and compresses. Comfort yields to constriction as the walls close in, squeeze down, and ejects the helpless body from its hallowed space. Pain intrudes; something beckons. "Move forward; leave this sanctuary," it urges and propels. Light and voices and fear fill this strange, new realm that inexorably forces alienation from the comfort of peace and darkness.

Faces appear, eyes focused on the tiny form shivering in the cold air. There is consolation in the new world with the recognition of a familiar voice and the warmth of touch. A new life begins, cradled in its mother's arms. A superhero is born!

PART I

AN INCONVENIENT TRUTH

CHAPTER 1

THE POWER OF WORDS

YOU ARE A superhero.

You possess the power of speech and your words bear tremendous influence not only upon yourself, but also upon others. How you think affects you emotionally, psychologically, and physically. Your words show the world who you are. They determine the relationships you have and express how you feel. Words define the world around you and your perception of it.

King Solomon of Old Testament fame wrote often about the power of words. He said, "Death and life are in the power of the tongue" (Proverbs 18-21 NASB). Words have the power to produce positive or negative consequences. They have the power to give life through encouragement and honesty or to crush and kill through lies and gossip.

I survived cancer. I know the power of words and a positive attitude. Throughout chemotherapy and internal radiation, I was determined not to let this disease get the better of me. I took one hour at a time, one day at a time, and, finally, conquered the disease.

I have now been cancer-free for ten years.

Let me ask you a question. Have you ever felt the blow of some words so strong that it pierced through your soul and left you emotionally wounded? The words of discouragement, the words of hatred and hostility, the words of unacceptability and complain? Those of you who have suffered the negative consequences of uncompassionate language can relate to what I am saying here. The loud voices of self-criticism, rejection and guilt in your mind often leave you apathetic. Criticism and derogatory remarks spoken to you by those around you leave you with the feelings of worthlessness, anxiety and most overwhelming guilt that invade your mind and continue in a cycle until you put a stop to it consciously and courageously. Doesn't it?

Words are unimaginably powerful. If you want to climb the Everest of personal excellence and create success in life put this power into play. Choose the words of prosperity, encouragement, possibility and compassion. One word in a day, focused fully and embraced wholeheartedly can make an incredible difference. Are you ready to soar higher in the realm of possibilities, where it's possible to allow health, wisdom, love, peace and prosperity to grow? Say the powerful word "YES" now. Answer to the call of personal excellence, "Yes, I am ready."

CHAPTER 2

LEARNING TO SPEAK

DESPITE CENTURIES OF scholarly discussions, humanity has come to no consensus on the ultimate origin of human language. Simply put, scholars have no evidence directly supporting any hypotheses. The subject itself was once deemed sufficient to exclude the topic from serious study until the late twentieth century.

Approaches to the origin of language generally begin from underlying assumptions, such as:

The idea that language is so complex that it

must have evolved from earlier, pre-linguistic systems.

The idea that language, because it is so complex, could only have occurred among humans in the course human evolution.

The idea that language is largely coded in human genetics.

The idea that language is cultural and learned through social interaction.

Fossil remains indicate that the capacity for language as we understand it emerged less than 350,000 years ago. Statistical methods estimate that vocal languages must have developed more than 100,000 years ago to have diversified and spread in the many languages and dialects around the world.

Regardless of when vocal language emerged, early speculative theories concerned its origins:

Early words emerged as imitations of the sounds made by animals.

Early words emerged as emotional interjections and exclamations.

Early words emerged as an expression of man's natural vibrating resonance.

Early words emerged from an attempt to synchronize collective rhythmic labor.

Early words emerged as sounds to mimic physical gestures.

Modern science dismisses those early theories as too simplistic; noting that the evolution of language hinges not on the mechanical capacity to make specific noises, but upon the arbitrary association of specific symbols to specific sounds. Children learn this with Dr. Seuss' 1971 cartoon *The Cat in the Hat*: "Cat, hat, in French, *chat, chapeau*. In Spanish, *el gato* in a *sombrero*." Animal sounds tend to be reliable; an animal can't fake the sound it makes in response to certain stimuli. A contented cat purrs; an angry dog growls

Human language is, ultimately, self-serving. We can fake it. Someone who is livid can still speak sweetly. Sarcasm gives meaning opposite of the words spoken. The meanings of words themselves change. Gay, which once meant "happy," now means "homosexual.

Advertisers and politicians manipulate language by purposeful omission of certain information to allow listeners to "fill in the blanks." For example, a politician will promise to cut the deficit, but not tell us how he intends to do that. He gives us information we already know—the deficit is too high—and says he'll reduce that by eliminating unnecessary spending. However, who determines which spending is unnecessary? What are the implications of those spending cuts?

Advertisers manipulate through implication. They use scientific jargon and vague claims to make their products sound credible.

Commercials attempt to sound unscripted, playing to the attraction of reality-based TV. They allude to the wonderful improvements in our lives by tugging at strong emotion: greed, pity, joy, lust.

Words fail the test of reliability because humans use them to deceive, even if only to maintain a polite facade, and persuade.

Another hypothesis, proposed in 2004, linked genetic interest with language. "Mother tongues" arose from mothers communicating with their biological offspring who then grew up and used the language with their own children. Shared genetic interest would have encouraged honesty and reliability in words.

That hypothesis led to another, "obligatory reciprocal altruism." Basically, high levels of intentional honesty fomented trust in the "mother tongue" among unrelated individuals to expand to entire tribes for the sake of cooperative survival and prosperity. That, of course, leads to social conversation and to ritual speech (e.g., storytelling, poetry, grammar conventions).

Other theories exist. Suffice it to say, science has not determined to its satisfaction how language emerged and evolved into the complex system of verbal communication humans enjoy today.

CHAPTER 3

THE SCIENCE
BEHIND WORDS

NEUROPLASTICITY REFERS TO the brain's ability to reorganize and establish new neural pathways to adapt to changing needs, whether that be recovery from trauma or learning a new skill. It's an umbrella term for the way the brain tunes itself to meet the individual person's needs and offers evidence as to the unlimited ability of the human brain to accommodate and expand upon the complexity of modern communication through speaking, writing, and gestures.

Etymology is the study of the history of words. Any high school English teacher can tell his or her students that English is Germanic at its base, expanded and refined by Romance languages (mainly French and Latin). Throw in some Celtic, Gaelic, Greek, and other ancient languages, and one gets the distinctive and constantly evolving mishmash we call English. Other modern languages share similar histories, even if their source words derive from different parts of the world.

Language evolves rapidly. Old fogies complain they can't understand what those young whippersnappers are talking about. Fifty years ago, there was no such concept as "internet" or "website." Two hundred years ago, no one would have used the word "genetic." Were two individuals in the same country, one from today and one from biblical times, to meet, they would not share the same language.

However, some standards remain, codified to create a reliable means of conveying important information. Science, for instance, relies heavily on Latin and Greek, considered dead languages, in the naming of new discoveries and for precise description to distinguish one type of thing from another. *Tyrannosaurus rex*, from the Latin, basically means tyrant lizard king and distinguishes a specific dinosaur. Any plant with *Alba* in its botanical name means it has something white—petals, leaves, stamens, or whatever. Any word ending in "ology" indicates that it is the study of something.

Words describe traits and ascribe meaning.

The observer principle applies to language as readily as it applies to physics. To wit: the observer's presence influences what is being observed. Words that land on the tongue may not be uttered or may be changed due to the presence of someone who is listening. Children speak differently to their parents than they do to their teachers or friends. Adults speak differently to their friends than they do to their bosses or their children.

Words convey relationship.

Words used in public can communicate vital, life-saving information, describe new inventions, inspire nations, or incite revolutions. They make you laugh, cry, fume, fear, love, and hope. They paint mental images of beauty and ugliness. They linger in the mind to influence and perhaps change or form a new perception.

Words have impact.

How do your words impact those around you? Do you treat yourself and others with respect, gratitude, and acceptance? Do you lift up others with a positive attitude or tear them down with negative words?

CHAPTER 4

WORDS IN PRIVATE

IN LATIN THERE is no word for *privacy*. Yet, our thoughts are private, contained within the realm of our own minds, hidden from view, inaudible to all ears but ours. The words used aloud and in writing publicly describe characteristics, assign meaning, and determine relationships. What do the words spoken within your mind do?

Self-talk[1] is described as anything you say aloud or within your mind that evokes emotion and is the primary source of feelings and

---

[1]   Oswald, MHT, MNLP, MTLT, Yvonne. *Every Word Has Power: Switch on Your Language and Turn on Your Life*. 2008. Atria Books: New York, NY.

perceptions being wired into our subconscious. Negative words and thoughts are associated with low energy; positive words and thoughts with high energy. Harmful, negative, low-energy talk is the most common. A key point to remember here is that the long-term effects of such talk can adversely affect our attitudes, dispositions and health when they trickle into our beliefs about everything else in our lives.

Someone who is always negative, who constantly complains, sucks the life out of the room. Does that little voice inside your head do the same to you? Does it tell you that you're not good enough? Not smart enough? Not capable enough? Or does that private voice that no one but you can hear tell you that you are worthy? You are loved. You can create anything you want in your life. Does it speak the truth or does it speak what you accept as the truth?

Wise men and philosophers throughout

the ages have disagreed on many things, but many agree with Ralph Waldo Emerson on one point: "We become what we think about. A man is what he thinks about all day long." Roman emperor Marcus Aurelius put it this way: "A man's life is what his thoughts make of it." In Proverbs 23:7 (NASB), we find, "For as he thinks within himself, so he is."

One Sunday afternoon, a cranky grandfather was visiting his family. As he lay down to take a nap, his grandson decided to have a little fun by putting limburger cheese on the old man's mustache. Soon grandpa awoke with a snort and charged out of the bedroom saying, "This room stinks." Through the house he went, finding every room smelling the same: foul. Desperately, he made his way outside only to find that "The whole world stinks!"

So it is when we fill our minds the negativity. Everything we experience and everyone we encounter will carry the same scent we hold in our minds.[2]

---

[2] Liraz, Meir. *The Top 100 Inspirational Anecdotes and Stories: A Collection of Witty, Inspiriting, Amusing, Eye-Opening and Spirit-Soothing Anecdotes and Stories.* 2010. ASIN B003XYFNU2.

PART II

THE INFLUENCE OF LANGUAGE UPON THOUGHT & LEARNING

CHAPTER 5

CHILDHOOD INFLUENCES

MANY PEOPLE FEEL compelled to give voice to any passing thought without heeding the significance of what they say or the impact their words have. Those words can leave a lasting impression on a child, especially an impressionable child.

If you look hard enough, you will discover a "character" in your family. Mine was loaded with them.

I grew up in my grandmother's house along with my parents, three younger brothers, and my mother's only sister. Nina, my grandmother, loved flowers and framed the yards with expansive gardens.

My grandmother's sister, Stella and her husband Bill loved gardening and would visit to tend Nina's gardens. When I was five years old, Aunt Stella, Uncle Bill, Aunt Nettie and Uncle George came for a visit early one balmy, spring evening. As the sun began to set, Uncle Bill walked out the back door and headed for the forsythia bushes that lined the back fence. Bored with listening to "grown-up" talk, I joined him.

I walked up to him and asked, "Whatcha doin'?"

"Just checking the bushes to see if they need pruning, Mickey Mouse," he replied. My mom's side of the family called me Mickey, my dad's side Shelley. It's a wonder I didn't grow up with multiple personalities. Or did I?

The real reason Uncle Bill had gone outside

was to smoke a cigar. He stood there, rolling that cigar around in his mouth scrutinizing the resplendent golden foliage. Slipping his hand into the inner pocket of his sports coat he produced a second cigar, and asked, "Wanna smoke?"

I told him I didn't know how to smoke. "You don't, he queried. Well I'll just have to teach you". Taking the lit cigar from his mouth, he handed it to me and instructed, "Suck on it like you're drinking from a straw."

As I closed my lips around the soggy end, a gush of amber colored juice trickled down my chin. With extreme apprehension I drew in the feculent smelling smoke and felt a sputtering of tepid, putrid liquid splash against my tongue resulting in a fit of coughing and gagging. Uncle Bill laughed hysterically and took the cigar back.

"Maybe you should wait until you're six before you start smoking," he said.

Once I was able to regain my composure, I summoned the courage to ask him about Aunt Nettie's leg.

"A snake ate it. But don't say anything to anyone. It makes them sad." "I won't," I promised.

Fast forward eleven years.

I found myself walking through a cemetery one crisp October morning, several feet behind Aunt Daphne, Nina, and Mom as they sauntered soberly through the leaves. My brothers followed behind me. One of them tripped over a grave marker and yelled. I turned to see what he was griping about and saw what happened. The sight sparked a memory of when I was seven years old. My Aunt had dragged me into a historical graveyard. She loved to read the epitaphs on the ancient stones. Mindlessly wandering behind her I tripped over a small flat stone and stubbed my toe. The marker was round and engraved with a "T." Racked with pain I somehow managed to ask my Aunt what it was. My aunt told me then it was a turtle grave.

"You need to be more careful around turtle graves," I told my brother.

When my aunt heard that, she stopped dead in her tracks, wheeled around, and exclaimed, "You don't really believe that, do you?"

"That's what you told me they were," I accused.

She looked at my mother and said, "You brought her into this world. How she managed to get to this age and be so gullible is beyond me."

I retorted that it wasn't my fault that I believed what my elders told me no matter how full of crap they are and added, "I suppose Aunt Nettie's leg wasn't eaten by a snake, either."

"Who the hell told you that?" she shrieked.

"Uncle Bill."

My grandmother had had enough of this display and requested quite sharply and vociferously that we both, "Shut your mouths and let me bury my mother in peace!".

We learn from our elders, from tips and techniques to family history and stories passed down from one generation to the other, just as Uncle Bill told me the story of Aunt Nettie's leg. We are predisposed to believe what our elders tell us, to take those words to heart and pass them down to our own children, one generation to the next and so on until stories become histories and accepted as truth. Because of this generational transfer and the belief our children give to what we say, the stories we tell have a substantial impact, which should make us more conscious of our words. Light hearted stories told in jest such as the ones told to me is a form of deception that left an impression on me. I grew up believing these lies. They weren't lies meant to hurt me, just light hearted deceptions but deceptions just the same. Didn't suffer any psychological trauma as a result but do remember feeling a bit foolish when faced with the truth.

CHAPTER 6

HOW LANGUAGE LIMITS US

YOU MAY HAVE heard that our brains are like a supercomputer, storing whatever is programmed into them. What do think happens when you think things like, "I hate that!" Or, "You're such a jerk." Or, "I will never get —." Every time you say something negative, you reinforce those self-limiting beliefs within your subconscious. The subconscious controls your life. These self-limiting beliefs are another form of deception that we tend to buy into. They become the truth we are willing to except rather than recognizing them for the lies that they are.

I once read that thoughts are vibrations which emanate in waves around you. Perhaps that's why, when you are around happy people, you feel happy, and when you are around depressing people, you feel down. New technology allows researchers to view the brain while it's working to learn about how our thoughts wire our brains. They're seeing neuroplasticity in action. Research has shown that your conscious intention to do something increases your brain's ability to wire new ideas. Concentrating or meditating on positive thoughts can be more powerful than any drug.

In 1973, Apollo 14 astronaut Edgar Mitchell, the sixth man to walk on the moon, created the Institute of Noetic Sciences. During the return trip to Earth, he experienced a profound sense of universal connectedness which led him to understand that there was more to reality than present-day science believed. In 1993, the

Institute published *Spontaneous Remission: An Annotated Bibliography* by Caryle Hirshberg, who gleaned statistics from over 3,500 references from more than 800 journals in 20 different languages. The research resulted in establishment of the world's largest database of medically reported cases of spontaneous remission, recording medical evidence of the disappearance of disease or cancer without medical treatment or treatment considered insufficient to cure the ailment.

ABC News published an article, "Positive Thinking, Faster Recovery,"[3] on the power of positive thinking, based on a review published in the August 2015 issue of *Canadian Medical Association Journal.* The review was written by Donald Cole, of the Institute for Work and

---

[3] "Positive Thinking, Faster Recovery," ABC News, July 24, 2016. URL: http://abcnews.go.com/Health/story?id=117317&page=1.

Health in Toronto, and spanned 30 years of studies that examined patient attitudes and post-surgery expectations. The review concluded that optimists fared better after surgery than pessimists.

"The review says the power of positive thinking is real," said ABC News' medical correspondent Dr. Nancy Snyderman on *Good Morning America*. She added, "This mind-body connection that we have been toying with for the past couple of decades really does have hard science behind it."

Further evidence on how the mind affects the body is given by Joseph Mercola, D.O. Dr. Mercola, who is published in the Canadian Medical Association Journal, the Journal of the American Osteopathic Association, and the Journal of the American Medical Association. He states that "[y]ou have had a longstanding deal with biology: whatever choices you make during your life might ruin your short-term memory or make you gain weight or could hasten death, but they won't change your genes—your actual DNA."[4]

Dr. Mercola supports the empirical evidence documented by scientist Bruce Lipton, Ph.D. in his book, *Spontaneous Evolution*. Lipton is the epigenetics pioneer. Epigenetics is the study of changes in organisms caused by alteration of the genetic code. "[E]nvironmental factors like diet and prenatal nutrition can make an imprint on genes that is passed from one generation to the next," says Mercola.[5]

---

[4] Mercola, Ph.D., Joseph. "Why Your DNA Isn't Your Destiny" (January 23, 2010) URL: http://articles.mercola. com/sites/articles/archive/2010/01/23/why-your-dna-isnt-your-destiny.aspx.

[5] Mercola, Ph.D., Joseph. "Why Your DNA Isn't Your Destiny" (January 23, 2010) URL: http://articles.mercola. com/sites/articles/archive/2010/01/23/why-your-dna-isnt-your-destiny.aspx.

Leigh Forston, author of *Embrace, Release, Heal: An Empowering Guide to Talking About, Thinking About and Treating Cancer*, says that "Dr. Lipton's research—and the empirical evidence of colleagues—is forcing the issue enough so that changes in medical-school curriculums [sic] are currently underway."[6]

The upshot of the research and evidence documented by Mercola, Lipton, Forston, etc., is that your mind can cure disease as well as create it. Even though your mind is neutral, you program it with your thoughts and beliefs. Some people get caught up in negative thoughts and emotions, which can manifest in their bodies as disease.

Although epigenetics itself may be only 20

---

[6] Fortson, Leigh. "Epigenetics," *Embrace, Release, Heal: An Empowering Guide to Talking About, Thinking About and Treating Cancer*. (February 7, 2012) URL: https://www.brucelipton.com/resource/article/epigenetics.

years old, the power of positive thinking is not a new concept. The Talmud, an ancient compendium of rabbinical thought, states that, "Where there is hope, there is life." Hope is a word for "positive expectation."

Other evidence of how the mind can affect us physically is the famous phenomenon of the placebo effect, first published in 1955 by anesthesiologist Henry K. Beecher, M.D. (1904 – 1976). After ingesting a sugar pill or engaging in some other form of sham treatment, people have reported relief or even a cure of symptoms *because they believed it would work*. Beecher concluded over a series of 26 studies he analyzed, that an average of 32 percent of patients responded to a placebo.[7] This occurrence is the direct result of believing that the treatment will benefit them.

---

[7]   Beecher, Henry K. "The Powerful Placebo," *Journal of the American Medical Association*. (December 4, 1955) URL: http://jama.jamanetwork.com/article.aspx?articleid=303530.

Alfred Korzybski (1879 - 1950) developed a field called general semantics and argued that human knowledge of the world is limited by our minds and our thoughts; therefore, people create their own realities based upon their life experiences, beliefs, values, and memories. The words they use to describe their perception of reality do not form reality itself. Reality, he said, is understood through our perception of it.

How would you feel if you removed all negativity from your private conversations with yourself? What if that little voice in your head spoke only positive thoughts? Just think of what you could accomplish without self-doubt limiting you! Perhaps, like me, you could find yourself standing before a crowd of people, talking to them, even though for almost ten years those days were spent alone with little or no one to talk to.

Complain, Complain, Complain!

It takes a disciplined spirit to endure the monastery on Montserrat in Spain. One of the fundamental requirements of this order is that the young men must maintain silence. Opportunities to speak are scheduled every two years, at which time they are allowed to speak only two words.

One young initiate who had completed his first two years of training was invited by his superior to make his first two-word presentation.

"Food terrible," he said.

Two years later, the invitation was once again extended. The young man used this forum to exclaim, "Bed lumpy."

Arriving at his superior's office two years later, he proclaimed, "I quit!"

The monk looked at the initiate and said, "You know, it doesn't surprise me a bit. All you've done since you arrived is complain, complain, complain."[8]

Exaggerated? Maybe. What if you were asked to share two words that described your life? Would you focus on the lumps, bumps, and unfairness, or are you committed to dwell on those things that are good, right, and lovely?

Benefit to you: If you are dealing with a chronic illness, then a positive attitude may be of great benefit in helping you deal with your ailment. As someone who has been through it, I hold fast to the opinion that a positive attitude will at least help you cope. We may not have control over our disease, but we do have control over how we react to it.

---

[8] Liraz, Meir. *The Top Ten Inspirational Anecdotes and Stories: A Collection of Witty, Inspirational, Amusing, Eye-Opening and Spirit-Soothing Anecdotes and Stories.* 2010. ASIN: B003XYFNU2.

CHAPTER 7

WHAT STORIES ARE YOU TELLING YOURSELF?

PEOPLE WHO LIVE life to the fullest create life. Others go through life reacting to the situation at hand. Those are the storytellers. I was a storyteller. I told myself that I was supposed to be *this* person, whoever she was. My dreams of a college education or of being the first female Jacques Cousteau did not matter because they did not fit the expectations of who I was supposed to be. Now I live with the consequences.

A crippling absence of knowing my own identity gave me an understanding that people learn to love like they learn everything else.

Processing the information—directly or indirectly received—forms our perceptions. This statement is not based on any scientific study, but on my own perception. It came to me the middle of the night. After sobbing uncontrollably, a sense of peace washed over me. There were no voices in my head, just a feeling that I was responsible for myself and controlled my identity.

I decided I would take responsibility for my failure in the disconnection between what I expected my life to be and the reality of what it was. I would purge my mind of negative thoughts and feelings and understand that the people in my life acted not from malice, but from their perceived belief of how people interact with one another. To use a contemporary expression, I put on my big girl panties. I adopted a life of gratitude for the experiences that molded me and learned to accept people for who they were as I wished them to accept me for who I was. I needed to give them the respect they deserved to live their lives if I wanted to live my life as I wanted. I recognized in myself a profound desire to lift up others, I felt an urge to build a retreat where people could come and refresh their spirits but a kindly monsignor counseled me: perhaps I wasn't meant to build a physical place. My experiences prepared me to build them up with words.

We all wear many hats throughout our lives. We are sons and daughters, brothers and sisters, nephews and nieces, grandsons and granddaughters. Some of us grow up to become husbands and wives and some of us become parents. We all make sacrifices for our families. The trick is not to get lost along the way like I did. We all tell ourselves stories from time to time.

What's yours?

PART III

METAMORPHOSIS

CHAPTER 8

MOVING BEYOND THE VICTIM MINDSET

WORDS INFLUENCE OUR culture and environment as well as our thinking. They form our perceptions, which creates our reality; a reality we have the power to change. They build our expectations and inspire us to achieve or deter us from the attempt. We are programmed to live up to or down to the spoken expectations of others.

Admonitions and expressions of others' expectations can feel like brainwashing. Women, particularly, are conditioned to put the needs of others before their own. I felt that no one cared about my feelings or who I was inside—people expected me to be what they wanted to satisfy their needs and desires. When I attempted to express my own needs and ambitions, I was met with a condescending smile or an attempt to placate me: "Yeah, that's a great idea, but you can't do that." (Another deception). If you hear that enough, it permeates your entire life.

I graduated high school at the height of the Women's Liberation Movement, an exciting time of change and changing expectations. I intended to go to college, but my boyfriend proposed and I settled into the traditional role of wife and mother, abandoning my dreams. I lived to support my family: scout leader, den mother, costume designer, makeup artist.

The kids grew up and moved out. I resurrected those faded ambitions and started college with a new goal: to get a degree in business management and advertising and then go into hospitality management with the eventual objective of opening a bed-and-breakfast. Life interfered again. My daughter needed a babysitter so she could work to help pay the bills. Then my son married and produced offspring. I embarked upon a 15-year career of "Mom, can you watch the kids?"

Whatever role my husband and children needed me to play, I fulfilled it and lost myself in the process. I began to question even mundane decisions, such as planning a simple meal. Trips to the grocery store made me physically ill with indecision: what if my selections weren't good enough? What if I spent too much money? Purchased the wrong brand? I struggled to decide which items to purchase.

Benefit to you: A life of gratitude and acceptance takes discipline and time to develop. However, with continual practice you will begin to notice that the negative, low energy stuff in your life will seem less intense and you will feel more in control and happier.[9] Stress will begin to disappear. You will seem more relaxed. Who wouldn't want that in his or her life? Imagine yourself waking up after a better night's sleep because you no longer toss and turn all night.

Today, everyone seems to need everything done yesterday and there doesn't seem to be enough hours in the day. More and more people seek ways to achieve peace in their lives. I have found numerous experts who agree that implementing high-energy thoughts and words into your life will help you achieve the desired effect you seek.

Choosing to treat people with respect may not, at first, get you respect in return. But I have found that, eventually, the change will be

---

[9]   Oswald, MHT, MNLP, MTLT, Yvonne. *Every Word Has Power: Switch on Your Language and Turn on Your Life.* 2008. Atria Books: New York, NY.

noticed. Remember, we cannot control the way others act, only how we react to their words and actions.

Words are the power within you. You can accomplish what you imagine: you have the power to have the relationships you desire with family, friends, colleagues, and romantic partners.

In order to achieve those changes, you must adjust your attitude and the language—internal and external—that supports those adjustments. Imagine what your life would be like if you adopted an attitude of gratitude, acceptance, and respect. How will your relationships change if you accept people for who they are and not who you think they should be? If you respect others' thoughts and feelings—even if you don't agree with them—will they reciprocate? How much stress, bullying, racism, and ethnic and racist intolerance would disappear from our lives?

CHAPTER **9**

MAGIC WORDS

ALTHOUGH IT IS impossible to remove all negativity from our lives, we can remove enough to develop a healthier, positive attitude. We all have low-energy and high-energy words and emotions.

People can be categorized by how they process information into four groups: visual, auditory, auditor-digital, and kinesthetic.[10] Visual people say things like *look, consider, contemplate,* and

---

[10] Ellerton, Ph.D., ISP, CMC, Roger. "Modalities and Representational Systems," *Renewal Technologies, Inc.: Helping You Get the Most Out of Your Life.* (2015.) URL: http://www. renewal.ca/nlp10.htm.

observe. Auditory people say things like *hear, discern, ascertain,* and *listen.* Auditory-digital people are self-talkers; they must be confident in the logic of some feeling or action before taking it. Kinesthetic people use words pertaining to feeling. They understand or feel what is being said. Since each group processes information differently, communication between people from two different groups can be difficult. Try to be conscious of this fact when you are in a difficult conversation and the other person doesn't seem to comprehend what you are trying to convey. Perhaps using the same language as that other person may improve your chance of making a point.

For example, if you are a visual person and you prefer to listen and speak in terms of words that are visually descriptive then you would have to change your way of communication for your auditory friend. He would not understand you clearly with your visually descriptive words. You would rather have to use more auditory words to get his attention and allow a smooth communication.

People actually like those people who can make them feel good and by applying this technique you can do this and attract people towards you. Persuading others or empowering someone will also become very easier for you if you understand what words appeal them. Even many inspirational speakers use some "foul language" to shock the listener. When the mind of a person is in shock it's very easy to infiltrate it and communicate the message powerfully. Yes words are magical. Media persons and every advertising personnel know and believe in this opinion.

Hence, if you ever wonder why somebody gets through people's minds very easily and you can't then notice the difference between your languages. The words they use must be appealing to the internal representational system of the people while you lack this skill.

Developing this skill can greatly improve your power to influence people, attract clients and make friends that you get to keep forever.

So what words appeal to your representational system? Developing self-awareness will allow you to be more aware of other's way of processing information. Being a human, you must communicate every now and then to receive and share information. It's the only way you get to connect with the people around you. So why not improve your communications by saying the words that can make you a people magnet?

In an effort to remove negativity, I have found that switching out negative language for more positive language not only greatly improved my disposition, but also was instrumental in attaining a more positive attitude and gaining a new perspective. This new perspective had enabled me to rise above the realm of complains, rejection and worthlessness and step into a new reality. My new reality was originated from the words of gratitude, respect and self-acceptance. These are the magical words, which have the power to transform your reality positively. Now what do you want to tell yourself? More importantly, what words you would want to use for yourself?

Here I must tell you, the words you use for yourself creates your self-image. The way you look at yourself and the level of your confidence can be improved if you raise the bar of your language by making it more positive. If you ask the most successful and fulfilled people of the world to describe themselves then you would notice the level of positivity they apply in describing themselves. It's the language that mostly distinguishes a successful person from an unsuccessful one as we refer to it in creating a life of gratitude, respect and acceptance.

CHAPTER **10**

WISDOM OF EXPERTS

SEVERAL TECHNIQUES AND schools of thought deal with changing one's attitude for the better. Neuro-linguistic programming (NLP), developed in the late 1960s by Richard Bandler and John Grinding, is the science that explains the relationship between mind, language, and body.

The upshot: thoughts affect us physically. For over twenty years, kinesiology (the study of the mechanics of body movements) involved testing muscle response to stimuli. Evidence finds that the relationship between body and mind is so powerful that one's muscles react to what is and isn't good for you. The body reacts to what is true and what is not. That means that your sensory awareness will allow you to rethink future decisions. Your sensory awareness will increase the more you use it.

You may choose to enlist the aid of a psychologist, counselor, mentor, life coach, or hypnotherapist. Each has his or her own approach to dealing with the interlinked effect of mind, language, and body. Their common goal is to take their clients from where they are to where they want to be. They begin with a discovery process, then develop a plan or program to implement the desired outcome.

On a personal note, be mindful of the outcome you want to achieve and don't be afraid to ask questions. I sought out counseling once for a specific problem and progress advanced as expected until I mentioned that my father was an alcoholic. Suddenly, the counselor's focus shifted and he seemed fixated on that fact. I later learned that he was writing a book on the effects of parents' alcoholism on their children. The result was that I wasted a lot of money.

PART IV

HEALING BEGINS

CHAPTER 11

OVERCOMING MY TREACHEROUS MIND

MY BIGGEST OBSTACLE to overcome was the incessant ramblings of my fractured mind. Petty fights, condescending words, and patronizing tones would penetrate my mind, darting through as though I were listening to a speech in fast-forward. I fought to eradicate them and replace them with more positive thoughts. I liken that struggle as akin to fighting an addiction to drugs or alcohol.

The next challenge was to become more compassionate and flexible when dealing with others while still fulfilling their expectations.

Yet another challenge was building the strength of refusal, to say, "No," and to stand up for my needs. I really needed to consider just how to do that and to be mindful of not projecting bitterness and resentment. What I thought was "just being firm" was perceived as resentful. Hearing that made me even more conscious of the power of words. I began to become very conscious of *what* I said and *how* I said it. I removed all accusing language and tried to think of how I would want someone to say it to me.

CONCLUSION

Since you have taken the time to read this book, you already understand the benefit of adopting a life of gratitude, acceptance, and respect. You understand how words impact that. Many authorities have found this concept has numerous positive emotional, psychological, and physical effects on our lives. You are a person of free choice. You can choose to ignore the information provided within, as well as the numerous motivational and inspirational speakers and scientists, or you can open your mind to new possibilities and embrace it.

You may not be able to leap tall buildings in a single bound or bend steel bars with your bare hands or fly faster than a speeding bullet, but you have power like no other being in this world.

It takes just one person to make a change, then another to see the difference and make the same change. Before you know it, your friends and family, their friends and families, and eventually whole communities will feel the impact and make the same change. You have the power to change the world.

Words; your words, are the most powerful force in the universe.

You are a superhero!

Printed in the United States
By Bookmasters